An Inside Look

Kathleen Rooney, SSJ

Saint Mary's Press®

The publishing team included Shirley Kelter, development editor; Paul Grass, FSC, copy editor; Brooke Saron, production editor; Hollace Storkel, typesetter; Laurie Geisler, art director; cover and inside image by Digital Imagery © copyright 2001 Photodisc, Inc.; manufactured by the production services department of Saint Mary's Press.

The acknowledgments continue on page 82.

Printed in the United States of America.

5505

ISBN 978-0-88489-710-1

Library of Congress Cataloging-in-Publication Data

Rooney, Kathleen.
    Sisters: an inside look / Kathleen Rooney
    p. cm.
ISBN 978-0-88489-710-1 (pbk.)
    1. Monastic and religious life of women. 2. Vocation (in religious orders, congregations, etc.) [1. Nuns—Vocational guidance. 2. Christian life. 3. Vocational guidance.] I. Title.
BX4210 R65 2001
255'.9—dc21

                                                        2001001798

To my mother, Patricia, whose own need
made the writing of this book possible.
A special thanks to Ann Edward Bennis, SSJ,
for her editorial expertise
and to Janice McGrane, SSJ, and Linda Robinson
for their steadfast assistance.
And lastly, thanks to my sisters
Pat Marz, Lynn DeAngelo, and Gerry Green
for their love and encouragement along the way.

Contents

Series Foreword

An old Hasidic legend about the mysterious nature of life says that God whispers into your newly created soul all the secrets of your existence, all the divine love for you, and your unique purpose in life. Then, just as God infuses your soul into your body, an assisting angel presses your mouth shut and instructs your soul to forget its preternatural life.

You are now spending your time on earth seeking to know once again the God who created you, loves you, and assigns you a singular purpose. Raise your forefinger to feel the crease mark the angel left above your lips, and ask yourself in wonder: "Who am I? How am I uniquely called to live in the world?"

The authors of the five titles in this Vocations series tell how they approached these same questions as they searched for meaning and purpose in their Christian vocation, whether as a brother, a married couple, a priest, a single person, or a sister.

Christians believe that God creates a dream for each person. What is your dream in life? This is how Pope John Paul II, echoing Jeremiah 1:5, speaks of the Creator's dream and the divine origin of your vocation:

All human beings, from their mothers' womb, belong to God who searches them and knows them, who forms them and knits them together with his own hands, who gazes on them when they are tiny shapeless embryos and already sees in them the adults of tomorrow whose days are numbered and whose vocation is even now written in the "book of life." (*Evangelium Vitae*, no. 61)

In spite of believing that God does have your specific vocation in mind, you probably share the common human experience—the tension and the mystery—of finding out who you are and how God is personally calling you to live in this world. Although you can quickly recognize the uniqueness of your thumbprint, you will spend a lifetime deciphering the full meaning of your originality.

There is no shortage of psychological questionnaires for identifying your personality type, career path, learning style, and even a compatible mate. Although these methods can be helpful in your journey to self-discovery, they do little to illuminate the mystery in your quest. What is the best approach to knowing your vocation in life? Follow the pathway as it unfolds before you and live with the questions that arise along the way.

The stories in this Vocations series tell about life on the path of discernment and choice; they remind you that you are not alone. God is your most present and patient companion. In the "travelogues" of these authors, you will find reassurance that even when you relegate the Divine Guide to keeping ten paces behind you, or when you abandon the path entirely for a time, you cannot undo God's faithfulness to you. Each vocation story uniquely testifies to the truth that God is always at work revealing your life's purpose to you.

In these stories you will also find that other traveling companions—family, friends, and classmates—contribute to your discovery of a place in the world and call forth the person you are becoming. Their companionship along the way not only manifests God's abiding presence but also reminds you to respect others for their gifts, which highlight and mirror your own.

Although each path in the Vocations series is as unique as the person who tells his or her story, these accounts remind you to be patient with the mystery of your own life, to have confidence in God's direction, and to listen to the people and events you encounter as you journey to discover your unique role in God's plan. By following your path, you too will come to see the person of tomorrow who lives in you today.

Clare vanBrandwijk

Introduction

"What is it like to be a sister?" This question has been asked of me and other sisters in various ways and by people in all walks of life. This book is my answer.

When I was a high school religion teacher, my most animated classes were those spent discussing religious life. My students, for the most part, had already experienced eleven years in Catholic schools, yet they knew little or nothing about the lifestyle of sisters. In my conversations with adults and in parish adult education programs, I found the same keen curiosity and lack of information. Conversations with people of other faith traditions were just as inquisitive and stimulating. When I researched books on Catholic sisters, I discovered that most are written for the professional reader. These experiences planted the seeds for this book.

For most adult Catholics, knowledge about sisters ended in the sixties, when religious life began to change radically. The fixed religious "habit" of sisters yielded to "normal" clothes; their ministries expanded beyond the traditional role of teacher, and they enjoyed more personal freedom. What was once clearly understood about the life and the place of a sister became less apparent in the years that followed.

Information for young people who never experienced the "traditional" sister comes largely from two sources—their parents (or grandparents) and Hollywood. Whoopi Goldberg cavorting in full habit in *Sister Act*, Sister Stephanie as assistant sleuth in the *Father Dowling Mysteries*, and the singing and dancing sisters in *Nunsense* are the mistaken images of sisters today. Adults, too, share this erroneous view. Fiction and reality have become so fused that the layperson has difficulty knowing where one ends and the other begins.

This book is neither a scholarly explanation of religious life nor a guide to a particular religious congregation of women. It is a popular presentation for Catholics and those from other faith traditions who want to know more about this lifestyle. The book offers an inside look but also an overview, a "bird's-eye view," of religious life. Although it is my story, woven throughout are the voices of other women who have chosen this life but who would have different experiences about it to share.

My own background gives me a unique perspective on this lifestyle. Because I was married and did not enter religious life until the age of thirty-three, I have experienced life in three vocations: single, married, and religious. I can relate to the curiosity, questions, and confusion about sisters; once they were mine.

One day the disciples of John the Baptist had been following Jesus. They asked Jesus, "Where are you staying?" Jesus responded, "Come and see" (John 1:38–39). Like Jesus, I invite the reader to come, "open the convent door," and see what a sister's life is all about.

How Do I Know
Whether I Am Called to Be a Sister?

Two roads diverged in a yellow wood,
And sorry I could not travel both
And be one traveler, long I stood
And looked down one as far as I could
To where it bent in the undergrowth;

Then took the other, as just as fair,
And having perhaps the better claim,
Because it was grassy and wanted wear;
Though as for that the passing there
Had worn them really about the same,

And both that morning equally lay
In leaves no step had trodden black.
Oh, I kept the first for another day!
Yet knowing how way leads on to way,
I doubted if I should ever come back.

I shall be telling this with a sigh
Somewhere ages and ages hence:

Two roads diverged in a wood, and I—
I took the one less traveled by,
And that has made all the difference.

("The Road Not Taken," by Robert Frost)

On which "road" have you been called to travel? God calls everyone to one of four vocations: married, ordained (deacons and priests), religious (sisters, nuns, brothers, and monks), or single. This vocational call is in harmony with and fits your unique personality and gifts. It is the most effective lifestyle through which you can serve others, achieve personal holiness, and find happiness. God desires your happiness. Many people find this happiness in married life, yet God invites some men and women to religious life, priesthood, or single life. The Creator knows that these lifestyles will bring happiness and fulfillment; however, some people avoid their call to a particular vocation because of fear or ignorance. My own journey to religious life illustrates this possibility.

*God calls everyone
to one of four vocations.*

I was born in 1950 into a Catholic family, went to public schools, and attended what were then known as CCD classes (sponsored by the Confraternity of Christian Doctrine). In these weekly classes, I received instruction in the Catholic faith. By the time I reached high school, my formal religious instruction was over, and my practice of the faith consisted of Mass on Sunday, the sacrament of Reconciliation (Confession), a rather childish understanding of God, and a simplistic prayer life.

In my senior year of high school, I met the man I would marry. He was three years older, had a management position in his company, and was quickly advancing in the corporate world. I was drawn to his intelligence, humor, and drive for success. We married less than a year after meeting. My parents opposed this marriage but eventually relented when we informed them that we would elope if they continued to disapprove. We married in the Catholic church after my graduation from high school. I was eighteen; he was twenty-one. This was *not* my vocational call; in retrospect I know that it was an infatuation. But it was the "call" I wanted to hear, and so I decided that I had "heard it."

The marriage lasted less than two years, and we divorced. I was hurt, depressed, and very angry with God. Why had God not taken care of us? Why did God not make this marriage work? I pointed the finger at God—after all, is God not in the business of answering prayers? For me God was the proverbial genie in a bottle: rub the magic lantern, say the right words, and out comes the genie god to do my bidding.

I was about to embark on my first lesson in adult faith. God's failure to "save" my marriage was the kickoff. With a childish desire for revenge, I was determined to show the Divine One *my* wrath! I stopped going to Mass, quit praying, and shunned the sacrament of Reconciliation. In my mind God was the one who needed to come to *me* and seek forgiveness for failing to appear and to rescue me. This mindset prevailed for the next seven years of my life.

What I had failed to see or even to consider is that married life is not the vocation God had in mind for me. Marriage is not the lifestyle that fits my gifts and personality. It would not fulfill me as a person or enable me to use my talents in the service of others. God is for me; marriage is not.

God did not abandon me; God respected my free will. God is not a genie. Just because I had made a wrong decision, God did not jump out of the magic lantern and change who I am or what my abilities are.

Here is a metaphor to illustrate the point. You shop for a pair of shoes and find a pair you really like, but your size is not available. Pushing good sense aside, you buy them anyway. Well, you have the shoes, but the walking is tough going. Because you can't change your foot size, you find ways to make the shoes fit—with insoles or stretching. However, the shoes will never fit right or comfortably, no matter how hard you try.

It is the same with your vocation. When you find the one that "fits," walking through life becomes easier. Not that you won't be walking into some difficult or challenging places, but your feet won't hurt on the journey. When you are living out the vocation that fits you best and is God's call to you, an inner peace and strength accompany you, no matter where life leads.

What are some indications that you may have a vocation to religious life?

What are some indications that you may have a vocation to religious life? The answers to the following questions are possible indicators:

- Do you have a regular prayer life? Are you growing in your relationship with God?
- Are you an active Catholic who attends Mass? Are you involved in some form of parish activity, such as singing in the choir, reading at Mass, teaching in the religious education program, participating in a youth group or other organization?
- Do you have healthy friendships with men and women alike?
- Are you someone who reaches out to others through volunteer work or simple acts of kindness, such as visiting an elderly neighbor or someone ill in the hospital?
- Do you have an increasing sense that something is lacking in your life? Are you looking for more meaning and purpose?
- Do you experience a deepening awareness of God and a growing hunger to draw closer to God, to the church, and to others?

Answering yes to all or some of these questions does not necessarily mean that you should be a sister, but it does indicate your potential for this lifestyle.

As for myself, I was twenty-seven by the time I could hear God's invitation to religious life. Jesus said, "The truth will make you free" (John

8:32). Up until this time, I had been unwilling to face my own truth. I was still blaming God for my failed marriage. Not until I honestly looked at my life and willingly took ownership both of my decision to marry and of the choices I made in my marriage could God bring me to healing and wholeness. Only then did my relationship with God begin to grow into one of love. God was no longer my enemy.

Soon I started to consider religious life. After getting over the initial shock of such a consideration, I made inquiries and eventually went on weekend retreats to explore this vocation. I also pursued an annulment of my marriage, which was granted. (The church, after a formal inquiry into a marriage, can declare the marriage null and void, based on events or conditions present before the marriage; a civil divorce must already have been obtained.) Over a period of time, I became certain that the vocation of sister was my calling, and at the age of thirty-three, I entered the religious congregation of the Sisters of Saint Joseph of Philadelphia.

Who Can Be a Sister?

I will later explore what I call obstacles to pursuing religious life, but if there are no obstacles, the following general qualifications apply to most religious congregations, in one form or another.

These general qualifications apply to most religious congregations.

Age

A woman between the ages of twenty and fifty is eligible to begin the initial stage of inquiry into religious life. Women today generally enter this process between their mid-twenties and early thirties. They have a career, a college degree, and established friendships, but they feel that something is missing in their lives. For such women only religious life will bring fulfillment. As Saint Augustine said, "Our hearts are restless until they find rest in Thee" (*Confessions,* book 1, chapter 1).

I was in my early thirties when I began my religious formation, the academic and spiritual program that leads to lifelong promises of poverty, chastity, and obedience. I don't regret entering at that age. Although I am grateful for all my life experiences up to that point, my life has never been as happy, as purposeful, and as graced as it has been since I became a sister.

Life Experience

Religious congregations today prefer women candidates who have had some college education, experience in the workplace, friendships, and dating relationships. Religious life is no longer what it was twenty or more years ago, when women entered the convent at the age of seventeen or eighteen. Early entry is no longer encouraged. An individual needs to have developed a sense of self and an ability to live a common life with other women in a committed relationship to God and the religious order. A woman cannot say yes to this lifestyle if she is not clear about what she is also saying no to.

Older women have had varied life experiences. Although it is not common, some—like myself—have been married and have obtained the annulment necessary before joining the religious community. Some women have borne children before entering religious life. In these cases the children must be grown, and the woman needs to be free of any marital commitment. A woman who has been sexually active can enter religious life; however, the vow of chastity does mean a life of abstinence from that point on.

The truth of the matter is—surprise!—we sisters are human! We come from varied backgrounds and life experiences. We are not born with a veil on our head and baptized in a black baby habit. We are women who at some point in our life realized that God might be calling us to religious life, and we explored this possibility. The more we searched, the greater the conviction became that this is the life we desire. We say our yes freely and joyfully.

We say our yes
freely and joyfully.

Obstacles to Answering the Call to Religious Life

Among the major obstacles to responding to a religious vocation are ignorance and misconceptions, fear, lack of support from family and friends, and previous life choices.

Ignorance and Misconceptions

Many people have little knowledge of what the life of a sister today is really like. Their information tends to be a mixture of myth, memories of sisters long ago, and Hollywood's version. With such a lack of information, they find it difficult to assess this lifestyle choice. Questions surface, such as: "You can't go home and see your family, can you?" "Are you told all the time what to do?" "Can you wear a bathing suit?" "Is your life boring?" All these questions attest to a lack of information and can certainly be obstacles to hearing a call to religious life. The answers to these questions, for most religious communities, are: "Yes, we can." "No, we're not." "Yes." "Definitely not!"

Fear

Fear of commitment is common in today's society. Many people fear the unknown and hesitate to take a risk, especially if the decision involves an eventual life-altering change. Although such fear is understandable, not addressing it is unhealthy.

I can remember my own fear when I first began to think about religious life. My concerns centered on leaving my job, selling my car, moving to another state—all valid considerations. But when a woman begins talking to vocation directors and visiting different congregations, she is still a long way from taking action. In my own fear and ignorance, my mind was jumping from a simple questioning phase to a committed life as a sister. I was not living in the present; rather, I was projecting myself into the future and imagining all sorts of serious decisions. I was overwhelmed, but over a period of time I realized that the process of becoming a sister is a gradual one. The journey is one of stages paced to the needs and readiness of the individual.

Exploring the possibility of religious life does not mean becoming a sister, any more than the mere thought of having children makes someone a parent. Looking into the possibility of a religious vocation calmly and intelligently is nothing to be afraid of. Meeting with a vocation director, asking questions, and making a weekend retreat on vocations are all smart forms of inquiry. No sister will be lying in wait, ready to hustle you off to the convent!

The love of God will never lead you down the wrong road.

The worst action you can take is no action. The love of God will never lead you down the wrong road. As Jesus said, "Do not fear, only believe" (Mark 5:36). The wise Chinese proverb, "A journey of a thousand miles begins with a single step," might also be helpful to remember.

Lack of Support from Family and Friends

One vocation director said to me, "I've yet to meet a young woman whose parents are not very upset by their daughter's attraction to religious life." Why is this so? Why do family and friends often react in horror when a woman considers this lifestyle as a possibility? One possible answer is the lack of accurate information, as if a person were to think that today's teachers, doctors, nurses, and scientists study and practice exactly as they did fifty years ago. Although these careers retain their basic elements, they look and function differently than they did five decades ago. The same is true with religious life: the vows have not changed, but other aspects of the lifestyle have evolved. Yet, religious life is the one vocation that people seem to "fossilize" in the past.

Another reason for the lack of support is that popular culture frequently sees religious life as a "waste" of a person's life. Marrying, having children, and living as a "twenty-first century single" are viewed as the only lifestyles that can bring real happiness. This view could not be further from the truth. Ask the thousands of sisters who live extremely happy lives and find fulfillment in their lifestyle. People who oppose religious life for a friend or family member need to answer two questions. First, are their fears and worries based on factual knowledge of this vocation? Second, whose happiness is really at stake here?

I recently talked with a woman who had been considering religious life and had spoken with her parents about her desire. They were adamantly opposed and even forbade her to discuss the topic. A few months passed, and one day the woman invited a sister friend to the house. When the mother saw the sister, she turned to her daughter and slapped her in the face. She had assumed the sister was there to discuss the possibility of religious life.

Yes, this is an extreme reaction, but women encounter active resistance in many forms—not as violent as a slap in the face but just as real and hurtful. These negative reactions create grave problems for women who feel attracted to the religious lifestyle. Parents and friends need to examine seriously and honestly their own attitudes toward this vocation. Lack of vocational support is a difficult obstacle for women to overcome, and sometimes they can't.

Previous Life Choices

One choice in life can preclude making others. My marriage is an example; I had chosen marriage for the wrong reasons. By the time I was asking myself the right questions, I was afraid to hear the answers. I had traveled so far down the path that it was harder and harder for me to turn back. In other cases a marriage has brought children into the world, and the parents have the responsibility for their care. A drug or alcohol addiction would be another hindrance to answering the call to religious life.

In all your life choices, is God still with you? Yes. Does God continue to grace and help you in your lifestyle? Yes. God's love and acceptance of you are unconditional, but God also respects your free will.

Your true vocation
is the one that will make you
most complete as a human being.

God, who cares about your happiness and well-being, chooses your vocation for *you,* not for God. Your true vocation is the one that will make you most complete as a human being. My hope is that you have not taken any irreversible detour. As Robert Frost wrote, "Yet knowing how way leads on to way, I doubted if I should ever come back."

How Do I Become a Sister?

Give me the wisdom. . . . Send her forth from the holy heavens . . .
that she may labor at my side and that I may learn what is pleasing to you.
For she knows and understands all things, and she will guide me.
(Wisdom 9:4,10–11)

The first step in becoming a sister is to find a religious congregation you are
comfortable with, one that fits or complements your own gifts, abilities, and
personality. When I began to consider religious life seriously, I wrote to
several congregations in which I thought I might be interested. They made
plans with me to come for a visit, sometimes for a day, other times for a
weekend.

During this search for a congregation, I found that some communities
are too structured and traditional for my personality. For instance, sisters in
some congregations can never be out of the traditional habit; they have little share in decision making, and their work is limited to one or two areas,
such as teaching or nursing. Other congregations I visited are more modern
in their religious lifestyle: they have equality in decision making, a deep commitment to issues of social justice, and no fixed pattern of dress. But some
of these modern communities didn't feel like a good fit either.

It was not until I visited the Sisters of Saint Joseph that I felt I had found my home. I liked the sisters I met; I was comfortable with their style of dress, their prayer, and their community living. Their works are broad and varied. I felt an inner sense of rightness that told me this could be the congregation for me. Thus began my eight-year journey to sisterhood.

People have frequently asked me in surprise and wonder, "You mean all congregations are not the same?" I answer, "No," and follow up with my own question: "Are all men or all women the same?" No one would say, "Just pick any man or any woman to marry—they're all the same!" Religious congregations differ as much in "personality" as individuals do.

Religious congregations differ as much in "personality" as individuals do.

Consider the following dating analogy to help clarify this search for the right congregation. When two people begin to date, they sort through all kinds of information, impressions, and feelings—some conscious and some unconscious. At times the relationship never goes beyond a few dates. With other couples a longer relationship is the result. Only when there is a mutual connection between the two people does a serious relationship develop. Without shared affection and care, only pain and heartache will emerge. The same process applies to a religious congregation and a woman: they must share a sense of compatibility and rightness. Among the many congregations to choose from, the one that seems to provide the best fit is the one to pursue.

When a woman finds a congregation that attracts her, she meets with the community's vocation director. In sessions that are relaxed and informal, they discuss the woman's spiritual life, goals, and desires. The director shares additional information about the congregation (its history and types of work), answers any questions, invites the woman to week-end retreats or days of prayer, and arranges meetings with others who are considering this same lifestyle. She may visit different convents of the order and join the sisters for dinner or stay overnight. This period of exploration and inquiry can last from a few months to a year or more, depending on the affinity between the individual and the congregation.

A good vocation director, however, will recommend one or two other congregations for the woman to contact if her personality and gifts seem better suited to them. Vocation directors are not "recruiters," but they are concerned with the rightness of this vocation for the woman and with helping her find the congregation best suited for her. If a sense of compatibility becomes apparent, along with a readiness and a desire to look more closely into the lifestyle, she becomes a postulant. (The name given to this and to other stages of formation may differ among congregations.)

Stages of Religious Formation

Postulancy

The term *postulant* describes a woman who is not yet committed to the congregation but is ready to live in a convent setting and to become involved in its works. Thus begins her religious formation, commonly referred to simply as formation: the spiritual and academic process that leads to promises of chastity, poverty, and obedience for life. This process involves several stages and is the means by which a woman can discover whether this lifestyle is for her and whether the congregation is the best fit.

The woman lives in a convent, shares in all aspects of community liv-ing, and is involved in ministry. This word *ministry*, which describes the work of sisters, has spiritual and religious implications. Because sisters consciously bring Gospel values to their service of others, they use the word *ministry* rather than *job* or *career*.

The woman, now a postulant, meets regularly with the director of formation, a sister trained and educated to work with women in religious formation. They discuss the postulant's prayer life and any questions or problems she may be experiencing in her transition into community living, which is not always smooth or simple.

Entering this new way of life can be difficult and challenging. An already established pattern of living and decision making does not disappear once a woman walks through the convent door. Living with other women, sharing decisions, and forming new relationships—these all involve struggle. The convent of sisters and the formation director, aware of these transitional difficulties, assist the woman in every way possible as she makes her initial adjustment to religious life.

Different congregations have varying time periods for the postulancy, but generally it lasts from one to two years. At any time during this period, the woman is free to leave the convent if she realizes that this vocation is not for her.

Finally I would live in a convent and see at close range what this life is about.

I can remember my own postulancy very well. I was to live in Saint Michael's Convent in North Philadelphia with four other postulants, joining eighteen sisters who already resided there. I had mixed feelings; I was scared, inquisitive, and very excited. Finally I would live in a convent and see at close range what this life is about. The five of us had picked our own bedrooms, unpacked our belongings, and added the small treasures and touches that would make these rooms our own. The bedrooms were very small, and I remember thinking, "Where am I going to put all my stuff?" My first transitional adjustment had begun.

Twice a day, the five of us prayed together with the other sisters. This vocal prayer, called the Liturgy of the Hours (the Divine Office), requires harmony and a regular pace. I needed to incorporate my voice into the blend of twenty-two others. This may sound rather trivial, but it was another adjustment among the many I had to make. It was no longer "I" and my pace of prayer, but a compromise with the pace of the others. My joy was in having a group of women with whom to share my life and our mutual love for God.

Along with learning how to live in community, ministry is an important part of the postulancy. This ministry depends on the abilities of the woman and the needs of the parish or community where she is living. Some postulants minister at a hospital or prison, visit the sick, or teach, just to mention a few possibilities. In addition to ministry, postulants attend weekly classes to learn about religious life, theology, and church history.

There is also time for fun and relaxation: going to movies and museums or packing a lunch for a picnic. I remember great times of fun and laughter with the other postulants and sisters. I felt a wonderful camaraderie among us.

Despite all the transitions and newness, I found myself feeling more and more "at home" with this lifestyle. The emptiness that had gnawed inside me for so long was slowly but surely dissipating. I had a growing inner peace and joy. Some of the postulants were having similar feelings, while others found the experience extremely difficult. Although we were all different, the five of us moved along our journey of religious formation to the next stage: the novitiate.

Novitiate

The term *novitiate* comes from the word *novice*, meaning a beginner; the postulant is now called a novice. The Code of Canon Law of the Catholic church specifies that the novitiate must last one year but no longer than two (canon 648). Frequently, but not always, the "motherhouse" is the site of the novitiate. The motherhouse can be compared to the White House as the hub and the heart of the congregation's activities. Sisters in leadership positions work there; many of them live there as well.

The first year of novitiate focuses intensely on the spiritual life and the meaning of the three vows of poverty, chastity, and obedience. Visits to family and friends are limited during this year, the only year in formation with such restrictions. (During the later stages, visits with family and friends are encouraged.) Much time is given to prayer, reflection, and study. An annual weeklong retreat is a regular part—a highly anticipated event—of the novice's life. Her prayer life is paramount, and she meets regularly with her formation director to explore more closely where God is leading her.

At the end of the first year, the woman is missioned (sent) to a convent where she will complete her second year of novitiate. (If a congregation has a one-year novitiate, the woman makes first vows at this time.) She has a full-time ministry based on her experience and educational background, and she attends formal and informal classes on religious life. At the end of the second year, she makes her first profession of vows: she promises to live for one year the vows of poverty, chastity, and obedience. She is now a temporary professed sister. If the congregation maintains the traditional habit, the woman receives it at this time; otherwise, the congregation presents her with an insignia to wear. This religious pin or necklace, designed specifically for the congregation, identifies the woman as one of its sisters.

Temporary Profession

In this stage the woman, although now a sister, has not yet promised to live for *life* the vows of poverty, chastity, and obedience, but she has promised them for one year. These vows are temporary; she will renew them annually for the next three to six years (canon 655). (Canon 657 allows for an extension in special circumstances.) At the end of any year when her vows expire, she is free to leave the convent and the congregation if she has determined that this lifestyle is not her calling. The congregation also has the right and the responsibility to deny renewal of the vows if serious concerns have surfaced regarding the woman's ability to live a healthy vowed life (canon 689). If she has renewed her temporary vows, the sister continues in her ministry, attends workshops and conferences on significant church and social-justice issues, and completes any professional studies she has been pursuing.

At the conclusion of the period of temporary profession, the sister makes final profession, that is, final vows. She promises to live for *life* the vows of poverty, chastity, and obedience. Final profession is a joyous and sacred moment in the life of the congregation and of the sister. Following the final vow Mass, each sister celebrates with family and friends, rejoicing in her commitment to Christ and to her congregation.

Of the five women in my group who began the postulancy together, two made final vows. Of the three who left, one is now married with two children, one is deceased, and one, at last contact, is living the single life.

I close this chapter with an anecdote from the Jewish tradition. The disciple Zyusha asked the rabbi, "How can someone as lowly as me possibly live like Moses?"

"When you die," the rabbi answered, "you will not be asked, 'Why were you not Moses?' You will be asked, 'Why were you not Zyusha?'"

A vocational call requires an answer.

A vocational call, whether to the married, the ordained, the religious, or the single lifestyle, requires an answer. Hearing that call, answering it, and living it faithfully matter most.

Chapter 3

The Vow of Obedience:
The Promise to Listen

The promises of chastity, poverty, and obedience are at the core of a sister's life. A woman's commitment to live this lifestyle is her response to having experienced God's love in such a profound way that no reply less than total vowed commitment will satisfy her. The same can be said of a couple who choose to respond to their love for each other through the vows of matrimony. Nothing less than total commitment will satisfy them. In both instances, be it a sister or a couple, love has seized them, and only a life commitment to the source of that love will ever be enough.

Although I will explain each vow separately in this book, the vows are connected and interdependent. The image of a three-ply cord is a good visual to keep in mind for understanding the vows. No vow stands alone; they are all related and intertwined. Obedience is the commitment to listen to the voice of God; poverty commits a sister to the freedom to respond to that voice; and chastity—a passionate love for God—motivates her listening and her doing.

Understanding the Vow of Obedience

"Morning by morning [God] wakens my ear to listen" (Isaiah 50:4). In their vow of obedience, sisters promise "to listen with all our heart and all our soul and all our strength to the living voice of God" (Donald Senior, "Living in the Meantime," p. 62) and in hearing that voice, to respond. Obedience is their commitment to listen to the voice of God, and they respond by continuing the work of Jesus in their own time. Sisters carry on the mission of Jesus by responding to questions such as: Who are the poor, the suffering, the alienated? Who are the blind and the imprisoned? Where are the sources of oppression and injustice in our world today? Sisters do their part in creating a world community built on justice, where all are cared for, no one is in need, and the Good News of Jesus is able to be heard.

If obedience is the commitment to listen to the voice of God, how do sisters "hear" this voice and discover God's will? This recognition can happen in many ways, all of them necessary for true obedience to take place: listening to God's voice in prayer, in the leadership of the congregation, in the local community of sisters, in their ministries, in the people they meet, and in current events. All these are vehicles through which God speaks not only to sisters but also to everyone.

Discernment and Obedience

Recognizing the voice of God requires prayer, openness, and discernment if obedience is to be the result. I consider discernment to be "thinking with God." Discernment involves more than just an individual's thinking about a possible decision by herself; rather, it means bringing this decision to God and considering it in prayer with God. The difference is akin to talking to myself and speaking with another person. Discernment, which is essential for discovering God's will in any given situation, is fundamental to the vow of obedience. Discernment can take place individually or on a congregational level involving all sisters.

Discernment is essential
for discovering God's will
in any given situation.

Sometimes a sister or the congregation can easily discern the best choice or decision. At other times a more complex and involved process is needed. Jesus spent entire days and nights in prayer, listening to the Father's voice, discerning his mission, and receiving the strength to carry it out.

Because the ability to "think with God" is vital to the vow of obedience, I will say more about how discernment takes place. (Excellent rules for discernment can be found in the Spiritual Exercises of Saint Ignatius of Loyola.) A personal relationship with Jesus, nurtured through daily prayer, is a primary requirement. A person who does not pray does not discern. To become familiar with the ways God is speaking, revealing, and inspiring requires time spent in prayer.

I have often told my students that they need to become familiar with the voice of God within them to know how God is leading them. The example I use is a phone call. If someone calls you on the phone for the first time—or even the third time—a mere "hello" may not be enough for you to recognize the speaker's voice. If that call were to come every day, you would soon recognize each other's voice very easily. It is the same with prayer. The more time you spend talking and listening to God, the easier it becomes to know God's voice within you.

Praying with the Scriptures is one way to recognize God's voice. Try reading a Bible passage slowly while noticing the words or phrases that capture your attention, and with those words begin a conversation with God. In discernment it helps to pay attention to what is happening in your heart, the feelings that are moving you, and to bring these emotions into your prayer. The events occurring in your personal life and in the larger human community will enter your prayer and help develop your discernment.

Here is a common discernment process that is rooted in a prayerful relationship with God: list all the positive and negative aspects of a given decision; do this for each option you are considering. The number of negative versus positive factors is not as important as the weight you assign to each point. Just writing down the plus and minus points is nothing to fear; the process adds clarity and helps you see both sides of a decision. Your thinking is "out there," so to speak, in an objective fashion. Interior freedom, an open disposition, and "stepping outside yourself" to consider the options impartially are all necessary for this exercise.

First, take your negative points and talk to God about them; say everything you're thinking and feeling about them. Then be still and listen to the voice of God within you. The voice may be clear, like your own thinking voice, or it may manifest itself by an image. The voice may come in the words of a song or in a passage from the Scriptures. God can speak to you in many, many ways. You need to be attentive to the voice of God with the ear of your heart. Praying over the negative points on your list can take a varied amount of time, from an hour to several days, depending on the person and the decision in question.

After this prayer experience with the negatives, pray in the same manner with the positive aspects of the decision. (It is usually helpful to allow a day or two to pass before beginning this second step.) When the process is completed, consider your feelings during both of the exercises. Where was the *consolation*—the feeling of peace or sense of rightness? Where did you experience *desolation*—the feeling of sadness, despair, or unsettledness? These feelings are important. The Spirit of God will always lead you to consolation if the choice is the right one. Talking things out with a mentor or a friend can also be helpful.

*As you grow in your life with God
and in intimacy with Jesus,
you will be more able to discern correctly
what you need to do.*

As you grow in your life with God and in intimacy with Jesus, you will be more able to discern correctly what you need to do. Of course, not all decisions require such a process; sometimes what you need to do is quite clear. Perhaps you need more courage or trust to make the choice, but God will give you this strength, too. As you step out in faith and do what you know you should do, you will experience courage, trust, and consolation building within you.

Here are two examples of how the promise of obedience operates in a sister's life. She is teaching in a high school, and one day she receives a phone call from a sister in leadership in her congregation who asks her to consider a change of school that will require her to move to a new area. She must seriously consider the request because this vow disposes her to be sent, as Jesus was, to those in need. By virtue of this promise, the congregation asks sisters to look beyond their personal desires and preferences and to consider the common and greater good.

The question then becomes: Is this God's will for me as revealed through the congregation's request? The sister must discern with an open heart and a willingness to respond. She brings this request to prayer and to discussion with others who can help her decide where God is leading. After her discernment she shares the outcome of this process with the congregational leaders. Their understanding is that the sister's decision has come from open and honest prayer in conversation with others and with the vow of obedience in mind.

The flip side to this example is when a sister herself begins to sense that she is being called to a change in the type or the place of her ministry. When this awareness occurs, the sister must explore this possibility honestly—and with God. If she believes that God is calling her to another place, she makes her request known to those in leadership, and they in turn consider the matter.

In these two examples, you can see that the vow of obedience not only involves mutual trust between the congregation and the sister but also requires individual discernment.

The following example demonstrates discernment on a much larger scale, when it is the congregation that makes a decision or determines a course of action. The example is a corporate stand, that is, a deliberate public statement or action that a congregation takes with regard to an issue of human concern and Gospel values. The entire congregation's position is involved, not just an individual sister's opinion. An example is opposition to the death penalty, in which case the congregation might join an organization such as the National Coalition to Abolish the Death Penalty.

The vow of obedience involves mutual trust between the congregation and the sister.

When the congregation is considering whether to take a corporate stand, all the sisters are informed and educated on the topic through informational mailings, workshops, and professional reading. Prayer, reflection, and discussion are vital to this process. When the sisters are sufficiently educated about the corporate stand and what it entails and have had adequate time for prayer and discussion, they vote. The educational and discernment process may require a year or more before any voting occurs.

If the vote on the corporate stand is favorable, the congregation as a whole begins to address the issue, for example, by writing letters to civic, political, and church leaders to inform them of the stand and to request action in their area of influence. By using its voting privileges, a congregation that owns stock in a company can vote for or against any proposals of the company that relate to the corporate stand. Joining in boycotts of certain products and using educational ministries to inform people are other ways to put the corporate stand into effect. In 1988, the Sisters of Saint Joseph of Philadelphia took such a corporate stand against the death penalty. Other religious congregations are doing the same.

You might ask, "What about the sisters who voted against the corporate stand?" Certainly this is a difficulty for these sisters. However, a congregation's corporate stand does not mean that a sister can no longer have her own opinion on the subject. She can, and she does; her rights are respected. She will honor and accept the position taken by her congregation, even if she cannot personally support it.

Obedience and Canon Law

Canon law has some stipulations regarding the vow of obedience. Canon 601 requires that sisters be obedient to their legitimate superiors in areas relating to their Constitutions. What are these Constitutions, and who are the legitimate superiors? Every congregation has a formal document, its Constitutions, to explain its nature and purpose and to address areas such as prayer life, formation, vows, membership, and governance.

Here is an excerpt from the Constitutions of the Sisters of Saint Joseph of Philadelphia:

> Both the exercise of the service of authority and our response in obedience are lived out in a participative and consultative manner. We bring to our obedience initiative, judgment, and personal responsibility.
>
> Each of us in union with the Congregation as a whole seeks the Father's will mediated through the word of God, the realities of life, the call of the church, and the needs of the world. In our response to the Spirit, we embrace both the difficulties and the peace of this call to obedience. (Nos. 87, 89)

The term *legitimate superiors*, in the strict definition, means the Superior General of the congregation, that is, its president and chief executive. The Superior General can delegate authority to others to assist her in upholding everything contained in the Constitutions. Obedience for a sister means that in areas relating to the Constitutions of the congregation, she will recognize in obedience marked with dialogue the authority both of the Superior General and of those whom the Superior delegates.

Such obedience presupposes maturity, trust, and openness on the part of the sisters and of those in authority, not mindless obedience to trivial requests. Sisters are not robots; they are not computers that need correct input for correct output. Nor are vowed religious like children, who simply need to be told what to do. The vow of obedience, for the individual sister and for the congregation as a whole, is about seeking and following the will of God.

The vow of obedience
is about
seeking and following the will of God.

The promise of obedience requires more than just a "Jesus and I" conversation. It is not a spiritual solo flight or the Lone Ranger's ride into the sunset. Obedience is listening to God's voice as it comes not only through personal prayer but also through the congregation's leadership, the local community of sisters, their ministries, and the events of history. Obedience is the yes that brings the works of mercy and justice to persons in need. Sisters practice obedience when these words of Jesus become their own: "I have come down from heaven, not to do my own will, but the will of him who sent me" (John 6:38). It is in this *will* that the promise of obedience for the sister and the congregation finds its greatest power to create a better world through service to God's people.

Chapter 4

The Vow of Poverty:
The Promise of Simplicity

> [God] has told you, O mortal, what is good; and what does the Lord require of you but to do justice, and to love kindness, and to walk humbly with your God? (Micah 6:8)

Many people mistakenly think that the vow of poverty is a promise to be literally poor, to lack the basic necessities of life, or if not to lack them, to live on the fringe of sustenance with "just enough." This is not what the promise of poverty means. One look at religious life today would tell you that sisters are not poor. They are one of the most educated groups of women in the United States; most have advanced degrees or certification in their field of service. Because sisters do not lack any basic necessity of life—food, housing, health care, or clothing—what *does* their promise of poverty mean?

By way of example, here is a summary of what canon law (no. 668) says about this promise. Suppose that a woman owns stock in a company. When she promises to live the vow of poverty, she may still retain ownership of the stock, but she can no longer be involved in any legal, managerial, or decision-making duties involving that stock. She must legally turn over the responsibility either to someone else or to her congregation. She can no longer receive the revenue from the stock. She is free to dispose of the revenue to whomever she chooses, or she may request that the income be given to her congregation, which would usually be the case if the congregation is the legal administrator of the stock. If the sister leaves religious life later on, the stock returns to her control. Lastly, she must draw up a testament whereby she wills to whomever she chooses any money or material possessions that may come to her before or after her death. Again, the inheritor can be—but need not be—the congregation. The legal requirement includes the relinquishment of goods and their revenues as well as a civil will for the final disposition of everything.

What does the promise of poverty mean?

Aside from the legal aspects of this promise, the vow of poverty also includes three components:
- Sisters will live simply.
- Sisters will share all things in common.
- Sisters will choose an orientation that is closer to poverty than to wealth, and by doing so, they will align themselves on the side of the poor.

(Amata Miller, "Vow Series: Poverty")

Jesus is the role model for this promise to live poverty in the way I have described it. He lived a simple life, shared things in common with his disciples, and aligned himself on the side of the poor. Jesus spent his life trying to alleviate poverty. He fed the hungry, restored people to health, took the side of the poor and the powerless, and confronted the oppressors of his day. The Gospel makes it very clear that all who would call themselves "Christian" are obliged to do the same. Many people do take this mandate to heart. They give generously of their time, talents, finances, and resources to relieve suffering and change the conditions that make and keep others poor and powerless.

Jesus is the role model for this promise to live poverty.

Sisters, by their promise of poverty, pledge to live a life in imitation of Christ. By doing so, they continue the mission of Christ to create a world where all people have the basic necessities of life and confront oppression in any form.

Jesus did not teach that goods and great wealth are bad in and of themselves, but he did teach that they can be a danger that blinds people to the needs of others and distances them from the Reign of God and its priorities. "Be on your guard against all kinds of greed; for one's life does not consist in the abundance of possessions" (Luke 12:5). "For where your treasure is, there your heart will be also" (Luke 12:34). Note the powerful parable of the rich man and Lazarus. The rich man is in hell not because of his great wealth but because of his indifference to Lazarus, the poor beggar (Luke 16:19–31).

In today's society we have clear evidence that Jesus' concerns are valid. People live in the midst of material extremes from abject poverty to obscene wealth. The rallying cry of the day is, "More, more! More wealth, more possessions, more power!" The gulf between the rich and the poor widens, and the poor become poorer. Lazarus is still here. This social context and the mission of Christ direct the vow of poverty for a sister. In this light she can look at each of the three components mentioned above: living simply, sharing all things in common, and aligning with the poor.

Components of the Vow of Poverty

Living Simply

Living simply means being content with the basic necessities in life, enjoying what a person has, and resisting the temptation to accumulate or have the best. How is living simply manifested in a sister's life? Consider the amount of money a sister receives for her personal use. In some congregations a sister submits an annual budget to cover her expenses for the year. Other congregations provide a specific annual amount that sisters use to buy personal items, clothing, and gifts, and for enjoyments like going to a movie or eating out. The amount varies from congregation to congregation but generally is between $500 and $1,500 a year. A sister must be prudent about what she buys—distinguishing needs from wants and finding less costly alternatives for having fun or buying gifts. If a sister is in need of a necessary item that exceeds her ability to purchase, her congregation will assist her financially.

*Sisters experience
the "pinch" of poverty
in different ways.*

Sisters experience the "pinch" of poverty in different ways. For myself one struggle comes from not being able to buy the type and quality of clothing I wore in the past. Hunting for bargains was not something I did; now it is my exclusive way of shopping. Much of my wardrobe comes from secondhand stores and thrift shops or from sisters who no longer wear the items. I have discovered a growing release from the need to be dressed in the latest style or to have a large wardrobe. However, in all honesty, I am not completely free of these desires or of giving in to them. Going through my wardrobe to give away items I no longer wear or need is another way I can make an effort to follow a simple lifestyle.

The vow of poverty is one place where I see myself slowly developing. Promising to live poverty does not mean that the sister does it perfectly from the moment she makes the vows. Living these promises is a journey into greater and deeper fidelity to them, but it is never perfect. God is not a vigilant taskmaster who notes down every less-than-perfect fulfillment of the vows. The heart's desire is what God sees.

How the convent is maintained and furnished is another aspect of living simply. Living comfortably does not mean spending lavishly. Before making any major purchase for the convent, the sisters discuss the cost and the need versus the want. If they buy a new piece of furniture, they give the old piece, if it is still in usable condition, to charity.

In my teaching experience, students often think that the practice of this promise of poverty is frightening, even repulsive. However, upon further examination they see that they too share in this poverty. How many people today can purchase everything they desire? How many have the luxury of annual vacations wherever they want, for as long as they want, without some concession to cost? What family does not need to budget, cut costs, do without, or do with less? Very few. What can others bring to their version of poverty? Perhaps the same attitude as the sisters do: possessions and wealth do not guarantee happiness and security, and the poor have a special claim on all who call themselves Christian.

Christians might all do well to put more trust in the following words of Jesus:

Consider the lilies, how they grow: they neither toil nor spin; yet I tell you, even Solomon in all his glory was not clothed like one of these. But if God so clothes the grass of the field, which is alive today and tomorrow is thrown into the oven, how much more will he clothe you—you of little faith! And do not keep striving for what you are to eat and what you are to drink, and do not keep worrying. For it is the nations of the world that strive after all these things, and your Father knows that you need them. Instead, strive for his kingdom, and these things will be given to you as well. (Luke 12:27–31)

How much simpler and more joyful all lives would be if everyone took Jesus at his word!

Another way sisters practice a simple lifestyle is by honoring the earth and by prudently using and preserving the earth's resources (Alexandra Kovats, "Reflections on the Vows from a Cosmic/Ecological Perspective"). The earth is a living organism from which everyone benefits and for which all must be responsible. With this concept in her mind, a sister's growing awareness and commitment to care for the earth lead to practical considerations about wise or wasteful use of water, gasoline, electricity, and food and about the importance of recycling. Congregations have joined forces with environmental groups to foster global efforts in caring for the earth.

Sharing All Things in Common

The word that is central to this concept is *detachment,* an inner attitude or disposition that sisters bring to confront the materialism of contemporary life. Sisters need to look at their relationship to things and see whether subtle forms of "attachment" are creeping in (Richard J. De Maria, "Poverty as the Embrace of Insecurity").

For example, hoarding, selfishness, clinging to a "special chair" in the living room, or being fixated on a certain time schedule are some behaviors that challenge the spirit of detachment. If a sister, because of the nature of her work, requires an expense account and personal use of a car (cars are usually shared), along with travel and dining expenses, her challenge is to practice detachment. There is nothing contrary to the vow of poverty in having these necessities for ministry, but the sister must be cautious lest these means to the end become an end in themselves.

Sharing all things in common
also means to keep the distinction
between owning and using things.

Sharing all things in common also means to keep the distinction between owning and using things. When the congregation sends a sister to a new assignment, she leaves her former convent and accepts what the new one offers. Sometimes the new convent provides more comforts; sometimes, fewer. The purpose of mission is to "be sent" as Jesus was, with little encumbrance of possessions. Because of the vow of poverty, the congregation can send sisters wherever they are needed to serve God's people.

The Acts of the Apostles (2:42–45) describes the basis for sharing all things in common. The first Christians pooled their resources and depended on the community for their needs. Religious congregations can follow that same example. The money received from each sister's work does not go directly to her. The congregation may choose to put the money into a general fund. In addition, whatever a sister receives from lecture fees, author's royalties, a pension plan, or Social Security goes to the congregation. Many congregations pay into the Social Security fund for their sisters. Because the congregations will be caring for them in their old age, the benefits go to the congregation, as do any pension benefits a woman may have gained before becoming a sister.

From these pooled congregational resources, every convent receives a monthly check to cover household costs and to provide each sister with her personal money. The pooled resources pay for education, health insurance, cars, vehicle insurance, and spiritual enrichment and retreat programs. Some of this money is also used to finance ministries that need to be subsidized. Congregations also make charitable donations; for example, many congregations make substantial donations to relief efforts when floods, earthquakes, and political violence occur. By sharing all things and pooling their resources, sisters are able to meet their own needs and aid the larger community.

Aligning with People Who Are Poor

The examples in the previous two points illustrate how sisters orient their lives toward poverty while meeting their own basic needs. How do they align themselves with those who are poor? Jesus is their role model. He stood with outcast, voiceless, poor, and oppressed people and spoke on their behalf. Practicing the Christian belief that everyone is a child of God does not allow for ignoring the weakest in the family of faith. Because of this belief, sisters choose to stand with poor people as Jesus did, and they try to change any conditions that cause human suffering. How do they do this?

Practicing the Christian belief that everyone is a child of God does not allow for ignoring the weakest in the family of faith.

One way the sisters combat human suffering is through their ministries, working either directly with the materially poor or indirectly to change the conditions that cause poverty and contribute to human suffering. Addressing hunger issues is an example of the advocacy work that sisters do. How can the resources of the earth be distributed so that no one need be hungry? With modern technology and resources that can potentially feed the world's entire population, why are people starving, even in this country? If starvation exists anywhere, is it Christian or even charitable to pay farmers not to grow food?

By standing with people who are poor, vowed religious apply whatever power they have gained through their education, their work, and their contacts. They join with other social action groups to end hunger in the world. On an individual level, volunteering time in a soup kitchen, preparing meals for the homeless, and contributing items to food banks are some ways sisters direct their efforts to end hunger.

Some other ways by which vowed religious stand on the side of those who are poor include the following:

- Being a voice for the unborn by taking part in the annual National Right to Life March in Washington, D.C.
- Opposing the death penalty, imposed on poor people and on people of color more than on any other group
- Speaking out against sweatshop factories that use child labor under appalling conditions

Numerous sisters and many other informed consumers now refuse to shop in stores that depend on child labor to make cheaper and more profitable products. Educating consumers about sweatshops, writing to executives of corporations that have been targeted by human rights groups for their use of sweatshop labor, and contacting members of Congress are ways sisters stand with these children and demand change on their behalf.

In a more personal way, sisters embrace the condition of the poor when they, like the poor, find themselves with no control over and no options in a given situation. For instance, when an illness drains all a sister's strength and hope for recovery dims with each passing day, she can consciously choose to unite this personal loss of health with the lot of thousands who are denied health care or are unable to afford it. This experience is an opportunity to pray with and for the sick poor.

When individuals, institutions, and agencies make decisions about a sister's work with no conversation or consultation with her, the results can seriously impact her life. This happens all the time to people who are marginalized and poor. When sisters experience being "invisible," voiceless, and powerless, they unite themselves with the disenfranchised and marginalized of society and realize more keenly what it means to be poor. This understanding increases their empathy and fuels their resolve to work for change.

A sister's gifts and abilities
are to be shared for the
good of others.

To see the vow of poverty simply as a lack of money or material possessions is to fail to recognize the full meaning of this promise. A sister's gifts and abilities are not her own; they are to be shared for the good of others and the earth. This is what the promise of poverty is about. The virtue of the vow is for all humankind to embrace. In doing so, everyone will be the richer.

Chapter 5

The Vow of Chastity:
The Promise to Love

I remember a conversation I once had with a college student. She had been commenting on the good looks of a man we had passed on the street, and I affirmed her conclusion by saying, "Yes, he is easy on the eyes." As a reprimand, she turned to me and remarked, "You aren't supposed to look at men that way!" I laughed out loud and replied, "I may be a sister, but I'm not blind." Her comment, however, again brought home to me how people assume what sisters should think. For this young woman, the fact that I could appreciate a man's looks was somehow contrary to being a sister. Promising chastity does not take away a person's sexuality or gender!

Canon law states that this vow "entails the obligation of perfect continence in celibacy" (canon 599). Sisters vow not to marry, and in this single state they promise to practice self-restraint by not yielding to sexual impulses and desires. By such a promise, sisters try to live the first and greatest commandment: to love God with all their mind, heart, soul, and strength. They give evidence to the fact that God is enough! The promise of chastity allows them to direct their power, love, and energy toward all people—not just one person or a select few. The vow also opens up a sister's life to know God's personal love more deeply.

The promise of chastity allows sisters to direct their power, love, and energy toward all people.

Of the three vows, this one causes laypeople the most difficulty. Two questions loom: "Does this mean you cannot have sex? If so, do you miss it, or do you regret not having the chance to experience it?"

I answer, "Yes," to the first question; the second question requires a more personal response. I can only give my own reply here: a qualified yes. Having been married, I know the experience of sexual intimacy, and being human, on occasion I miss this expression of my sexuality. However, I am not consumed with thoughts about this "lack" in my life.

The truth is that a sister falls in love with Christ. This love is as real and powerful and consuming as it is for a married couple. Love for Christ and the intimacy of this relationship are at the heart of the promise of chastity and, in fact, of all three vows. This love compels sisters to make their commitment to Christ joyfully, knowingly, and freely. Love is at the core.

In my own life there was a time when this love was not at my core. In the years following my divorce, I enrolled in college and took on numerous jobs to pay for my education: cocktail waitress, bank teller, office worker, and receptionist; eventually, with my academic degree I obtained a position as a social worker in a hospital. The men I dated were as varied as my jobs—from professional businessmen to a man associated with the Mafia. Through all these experiences—jobs, relations, education—I was trying to find my center, something that would complete me. Yet, I was not fulfilled intellectually, emotionally, or professionally. The hollow center remained.

These final lines of Francis Thompson's poem, "The Hound of Heaven," state a truth that was then still eluding me:

Is my gloom, after all,
Shade of His hand, outstretched caressingly?
"Ah, fondest, blindest, weakest,
I am He Whom thou seekest."

The following event allowed me to "see" the outstretched, caressing hand of God: the Divine finally took center—fulfilling me, empowering me, and loving me as no one and nothing had been able to do before.

It began when two of my sisters in my own family became involved, a couple of years earlier, in the Catholic charismatic movement, which stresses both a personal relationship with Jesus Christ and the gifts of the Holy Spirit as outlined in First Corinthians 12:14. During that period, I witnessed significant changes in them. Their happiness no longer depended on the events of the day, the moods of their spouses, or how well their children were behaving. A quality of peace was ever present. This was quite a change from my pre-charismatic sisters! I was skeptical; surely this new behavior would not last. Despite normal ups and downs, problems, and difficulties, their peace and joy remained.

One day while driving home from work, I was thinking about the changes in my sisters. I knew the source was in their relationship with God. I was becoming slightly envious of them, and I recall saying to myself, "I wish I had that kind of relationship with God." This was the thought that opened the door for God to come in.

My twin sister invited me to go to a prayer meeting with her. It was a Friday night, and I wanted to go out to a club with my friends. But they had other plans, and I found myself facing a boring evening, so I said, "Yes," to my sister.

The prayer meeting opened with three songs. I was sitting, head bowed—not out of reverence but out of embarrassment. I hoped no one there knew me! With eyes closed I sat, and then Jesus came to me. I saw him in my mind's eye, his arms opened wide, looking at me with tenderness and compassion. He said, "Kathy, come to me." It is impossible to describe the intensity of emotion that swept over me; I began to cry. It was as if a dam had broken. I was overwhelmed with the knowledge of God's love for me. I wept throughout the entire prayer meeting, which lasted more than two hours. I can remember little else of what happened during the remainder of the meeting, but engraved in my memory is this vision of Jesus and his words to me. He changed my life.

I was overwhelmed with the knowledge of God's love for me.

I returned home, and this overriding sense of love and calm never left me. I awoke the next morning feeling very different. Within a week I had purchased a Bible and was conversing with Jesus with an intimacy and ease that astounded me. I could not get enough. I went to those Friday night prayer meetings for the next five years. I eventually returned to Mass and to the sacrament of Reconciliation. I read the Bible; I prayed daily.

"So if anyone is in Christ, there is a new creation; everything old has passed away; see, everything has become new!" (2 Corinthians 5:17) This is what happened to me. The "old life" was leaving, and the new life was filling me. My love relationship with Christ had begun.

Six years after this conversion experience, I joined the Sisters of Saint Joseph. Certainly not everyone who attends Catholic charismatic prayer meetings becomes a sister, a brother, or a priest. If that were the case, communities and rectories would be bulging with men and women! But the prayer meeting was what God used in my case.

When I first considered being a sister, I assumed that the promise of chastity meant no more male friendships, very limited family contact, and female friendships restricted to other sisters. My understanding of chastity was incorrect. At one time this was the way the promise of chastity was lived, in the belief that such limited relationships would foster deep love for God and increased personal holiness. Religious life at that time did not reflect the reality that all human relationships have the potential to make sisters holier, happier, and more Christlike. Formerly, restricting these relationships impeded personal growth. The changes that began in religious life in the 1960s attempted to correct this misunderstanding of the vow. The promise of chastity *does not* prohibit human love and friendship; rather, it insists on them. When I learned the truth about the promise of chastity, I was ecstatic and relieved! So, too, I might add, were my family and friends.

All human relationships have the potential to make sisters holier, happier, and more Christlike.

To promise chastity requires a willingness to love and to be loved. However, self-discipline and limits are understood in these relationships. Are these boundaries not true for everyone if relationships are to be life-giving rather than harmful? Like most sisters, I have close friendships with men and women, both religious and lay. I value these relationships and need them in my life, but they remain chaste. Although sisters have promised to remain unmarried, they continue to have loving relationships in their lives.

This brings up the topic of procreation, the human need to give and foster life. Sisters will not bear and raise children of their own; for some this brings a keen sense of loss. In the years before a sister makes the promise of chastity for *life*, this struggle may become problematic, and the woman may realize that she is not called to this lifestyle. The question has to be looked at honestly and openly for the woman's best interest.

This does not guarantee, however, that at times she will not be reminded about the real sacrifices she has made. Watching a romantic couple, a family enjoying time together, or a woman holding her child—these times of awareness come to all sisters. Prayer and sharing emotions with friends are ways sisters handle these experiences, which can be a means to look again at their commitment, the "why" of their choice, and to recommit themselves to the yes of their vowed relationship with Christ.

Other women may come to realize that religious life will not bring them the fulfillment they seek, and they leave—a choice, made in personal honesty, that is the best decision for them. A woman does not need to be a sister to live a life of faith. Many lead lives committed to Jesus and the Gospel within a family and make significant contributions in creating a better world.

To give and foster life is not limited to families or to bearing children. How often is life fostered by helping individuals overcome an addiction, by supporting them in their journey to recovery, by training people in a skill that will bring them out of poverty and restore their self-esteem, by helping abused women break the cycle of victimization and restore their sense of worthiness and value? Examples like these abound in the fostering of life that goes on daily in thousands of cities by those who are committed to love of neighbor without distinction. Sisters do not bear children, but they can give and foster life.

Personal Skills

Certain personal skills are necessary for living this promise of chastity in a healthy way. These skills certainly are not restricted to sisters, but they are essential for a sister's life (Martin Pable, "Skills Needed for Celibacy"):

- *Self-knowledge:* Knowing oneself deeply, accepting and liking the person one is, being aware of one's motivations, likes, desires and weaknesses. Religious life is no longer a vocation to "grow up" in, as in years past when young women entered in their teens. A woman must already possess a mature sense of identity to some degree. This is not to deny that people are always in process; change, growth, and development are a part of life no matter at what age.

Change, growth, and development are a part of life no matter at what age.

- *Capacity for solitude:* Being able to enjoy one's own company and to renew one's inner self, be it through prayer, music, reading, or painting. Loneliness exists in every lifestyle, but for a sister perhaps more so. Sisters can transform loneliness into solitude when they invite God into it. They need to have the inner resources to accept these times and to invite God into them. Running from loneliness or finding inappropriate compensating behaviors to avoid these times will ultimately lead to unhappiness. Nurturing solitude can bring self-discovery, inner strength, and peace.
- *Friendships:* Having a network of friends. Friendships with people of both genders and of different ages, backgrounds, and cultures are vital bonds that sustain and enrich a sister's life.
- *Positive view of sexuality:* Valuing sexuality as an expression of the total personality. Part of sexuality is expressed in a person's sexual orientation. For most religious congregations, the ability to live the promise of chastity faithfully is the issue, not the person's sexual orientation. Arriving at peaceful ownership of sexual orientation, be it homosexual or heterosexual, is necessary for everyone.

This list is certainly not exclusive, but these four skills are necessary to live a life of delight, fullness, and faithfulness in the promise of chastity.

Summary of the Promises

The three vows tend to be viewed often as promises of "cannots." I invite you to consider another viewpoint: these promises are resplendent with the *positive*. I am free to love *all* people with an undivided heart. I am free to travel and serve wherever in the world I have been asked to go. I am free to listen and respond to the voice of Christ in the poor and needy. I am free of the societal pressures of materialism, consumerism, power, and self-aggrandizement. I have been freed. The focus of the promises is not what I cannot do but what I have been freed to do. In my own life I can only say that this freedom has brought me tremendous energy, inner peace, joy, and growth in my own giftedness that I never thought possible. I have met, worked with, and served wonderful people. My commitment to the God of love has expanded, not diminished, my life.

The focus of the promises is not what I cannot do but what I have been freed to do.

Chapter 6

Behind Convent Doors:
What Living in a Convent Is Like

"For where two or three are gathered in my name, I am there among them." (Matthew 18:20)

People often wonder what it is like to live in a convent. This chapter "opens the door" and gives you a look. The term *community* refers to sisters who live together in the same convent; however, community life goes far beyond simply residing together in the same dwelling. Sisters share a bond, a love, and a faith that transcend any four walls. Living with other sisters is a source of faith, strength, comfort, growth, and companionship. Sisters share life in many ways, such as prayer, celebrations, meetings, having fun together, and keeping the convent in order.

In my naïveté, before I knew anything about religious life, I assumed that sisters spent their convent time in prayer, silence, and "holy" endeavors. I had this image of women who moved with such grace and goodness that they could almost be seen as "floating." I heard them speaking to each other in sacred whispers. I believed they prayed most of the day and night, except for the few hours they took to sleep. This vision was quite unreal;

nonetheless, it is the image many people harbor today. I will try to put this illusion to rest.

God has called the sisters to this vocation. They may have the same weaknesses and foibles as any other person, but sisters also have personal gifts and strengths. What joins them in community is their love for Christ and their vowed commitment to live poverty, chastity, and obedience while supporting one another along the way.

"So," you ask, "what is a sister's life like within the convent walls?" Come and see!

Communal Prayer

Our prayer is in common; we join together to pray the liturgy of the hours daily. Our Divine Office prayer book contains psalms, other scriptural readings, petitions, and songs. We pray the Office at different times of the day. We praise and glorify God, and God hears our petitions.

The prayerful recitation of the Divine Office is a means of offering the day to God.

Active congregations (sisters) pray the Office in common twice a day, morning and evening. The prayerful recitation of the Divine Office is a means of offering the day to God. Contemplative orders (nuns) pray this prayer of the church five to seven times a day, with different psalms and readings for each of the "hours."

All vowed religious, men and women alike, and all ordained priests and deacons pray the Office. Because this is the common prayer of the church, more and more married and single people are adopting it as a component of their personal prayer.

Mass

Sisters attend daily Mass as well as Sunday liturgy. In celebrating Mass we join with other members of the church to give thanks and praise to God, to listen to God's voice in the Scriptures, and to let that "voice" nourish, guide, and shape us. The core of our life is this meeting with Jesus in the Eucharist.

Faith Sharing

Some communities of sisters gather periodically, perhaps weekly or monthly, for an informal sharing of faith. The focal point can be the Scriptures, a personal reflection, or a discussion about their life journey at the moment. In my community we might address a struggle, a joy, an event, or how God is speaking to us personally. This way of talking together not only deepens our appreciation and understanding of one another but helps us keep in mind the many ways God is present in our lives.

Personal Prayer

This is the time sisters give to their own private and intimate conversation with God. Couples with children, with all their responsibilities of caring for the family and the household, need time alone, which is vital to the growth of their love. They can talk about significant issues, about the day, or just sit quietly with no need for words. Private prayer for us sisters is similar—a time when we can get away from the hustle and bustle of life and be alone with God. Neglecting this part of our life with Christ will in the long run weaken our religious life. When a husband and wife never find the time to be alone together, that neglect can eventually weaken their marriage. In the same way our personal prayer time is indispensable for our relationship with God.

The Convent

Another question people ask is, "What does the inside of a convent look like?" Convents have no definitive "look." They vary in size from small to large. Each convent has a kitchen, a dining room, a laundry, a living room (usually referred to as the community room), a bedroom for each sister, bathrooms, and a chapel. (A smaller version of a church, the chapel within a convent is not a public worship space for the parish.) Some convents may also have a small sitting room, a cellar, a pantry, a porch, extra bedrooms, and an office. As with any home, all these areas need care and cleaning. Each sister chooses an area to be responsible for; this is then known as her "charge." Sisters select these charges in dialogue with one another. An older sister, for instance, may take a charge that is less physically taxing; a sister whose work requires travel may select an area of responsibility that does not need daily cleaning.

Cooking

Besides their charge, sisters each take a turn cooking according to a schedule. The meal selected is the one she knows how to cook best. Some communities, depending on the desires and decisions of the sisters in the convent, choose to use a portion of their household budget to hire a cook for part of the week.

Shopping

Shopping for groceries is another shared task—one, I might add, that is my least favorite! We take turns doing the shopping, and if the community is large, we usually pair up. In my first convent, with twenty-two sisters, food shopping took on colossal proportions. People in the checkout line would stare in amazement (and dismay if they were unlucky enough to be next in line) at the volume of food being purchased. If I explained, rather sheepishly, that I was buying for a convent, their interest in our food order became intense. Miraculously, their boring wait became quite fascinating! I eventually stopped explaining the reason for this quantity of food, smiled sweetly, and let their imaginations run wild!

Meetings

On a regular basis, sisters meet to discuss, plan, and decide on various matters affecting their life together. The topics can range from the simple task of signing up for a charge or a cooking turn to a complex matter such as taking a public position on an issue of social justice. For instance, if a congregation is considering taking a corporate stand, the sisters need to be educated on the issue and its implications and need to be in honest dialogue about it. These meetings are often stimulating, challenging, and informative, but not always easy. Opinions can differ widely and strongly, but the community must hear, respect, and consider each sister's thinking. Convent meetings, called house meetings, may occur weekly, bi-monthly, or monthly. The frequency depends on the size of the community and the issues needing discussion. A convent of four sisters can discuss many topics informally at the dinner table; for eighteen sisters this would be difficult, and a formal meeting structure would be better.

Celebrations

Do sisters have fun together? Of course! All work and no play makes for a dull sister! Individual celebrations are held for birthdays or to honor a sister's accomplishment, such as an academic degree; general celebrations are held on holidays and holy days. Food, drink, and music mingle with laughter and conversation to make for a good time. In our convent life, we find time to celebrate in these lighthearted ways because we enjoy them and realize their importance. Life cannot be merely a succession of meetings, work, prayer, and domesticity. We need time to laugh together, enjoy one another's company, and relish some shared free time.

Daily Life

Along with the activities described thus far, there is the normal "stuff" of daily life. We enjoy watching television, playing cards, and chatting in the kitchen over a cup of coffee; someone else might be doing laundry, grading test papers, or praying in chapel. Going to a movie, shopping, seeing family and friends, and eating out are usual activities. The days get filled very quickly. Contrary to common opinion, sisters are seldom bored.

Conflict

Problems are a normal occurrence in community life. Although sisters share their love for God and their congregation, they do not always agree or see things in the same light. Sometimes they find themselves in opposing camps of thought or opinion. As a human, I may not like every sister in the convent. Individual idiosyncrasies can be grating. Sisters strive for self-control and graciousness; however, despite their best efforts, they sometimes fail. I offer myself as a case in point.

Problems are a normal occurrence in community life.

I was living in a rather large community at the time, and a clash of personalities arose between another sister and me. We both recognized this conflict but did our best to keep our relationship amicable. One day, what began as a minor disagreement escalated into a full-blown argument. We both said things in the heat of anger. Days and weeks passed with a frostiness between us that could have frozen a snowball on a hot summer day. Eventually, we were able to sit down in private, discuss the flare-up, and be honest with each other without the emotion of anger. Although we cleared the air, our relationship never did return to the amicable one we had enjoyed earlier, but we were polite toward one another. We no longer live in the same community, and when we see each other at various functions, the politeness continues. This social courtesy is the best we can manage.

I share the following story to exemplify community life at its best—and in the worst of times. It was the day my father died. I was at dinner with my community and chatting about the events of the day when the phone call came. I remember hearing my mother tell me the awful news. In that instant my world changed; I felt as if I were having an out-of-body experience. I observed the conversations still going on at the dinner table, and it seemed as if I were watching a silent movie.

After my phone conversation with my mom ended, I returned to the table and told the sisters that my father had just died. There was a stunned silence. Then these twelve wonderful women became one body of comfort, compassion, and help. They hugged me, cried with me, and offered me words of solace. They began to be my mind and my actions. Someone went to call my friends. Another made my plane reservations to Florida. I was able to call my sisters and other family members and talk with them in the privacy of our grief, knowing that the sisters in my community were taking care of the many necessary details. Later, someone helped me pack. Others went to the chapel to pray. Quietly and reverently, every sister came to my need in some way.

I cannot imagine what this experience would have been like without them at my side. This is community. I will always remember this event with deep gratitude. In this remembrance of intense loss and grief, another memory emerges—the sisters reaching out to me in love and giving me the support and consolation I so desperately needed.

I experienced the compassion and care of the women I had chosen to join on this journey of life.

Later, the congregation scheduled a Mass for my father. Once again, I experienced the compassion and care of the women I had chosen to join on this journey of life. This is community; this is Christ's presence with someone in her darkest hour.

What Do Sisters Do?

> The Spirit of the Lord is upon me, because he has anointed me to bring good news to the poor. He has sent me to proclaim release to the captives and recovery of sight to the blind, to let the oppressed go free, to proclaim the year of the Lord's favor. (Luke 4:18–19)

Christians are called to be the Body of Christ in the world today. Evils such as racism, poverty, sickness, oppression, genocide, alienation, and homelessness prevent people from fully realizing their human dignity as children of God. The "year of the Lord's favor" still needs to be proclaimed and actualized in today's world. God has charged all Christians with the solemn responsibility to be the hands, the feet, the eyes, and the heart of Christ in a world that is suffering today.

I can paraphrase Edmund Burke's famous words by saying, "The only thing necessary for the triumph of evil is for good people to do nothing." No one person, not even one religious congregation of sisters, can relieve the suffering of the masses, but as Mother Teresa advised, people *can* love and serve one person at a time. They can also join together with other individuals and groups to eliminate the conditions that cause human misery in the world.

Vowed religious make
a public commitment to continue
the redemptive work of Jesus.

Vowed religious make a public commitment to continue the redemptive work of Jesus. Religious congregations participate in this work and base their decisions on the particular mission of their founder. Mother Teresa's congregation, the Missionaries of Charity, was started for the express purpose of giving direct assistance to the poor. Other congregations have specific missions such as health care, education, and foreign mission work. The ministries of the sisters reflect the purpose of their congregation's existence.

Types of Ministry and Advocacy

Ministry for sisters takes many forms. They serve in all aspects of health care and human services as nurses, doctors, physician's assistants, social workers, counselors, lawyers, psychiatrists, home health care aides, and emergency medical technicians. They are also involved in the spiritual ministries of retreat work, renewal, spiritual direction, and worship planning. Sisters work in these ministries in the inner cities and suburbs of the United States, in Appalachia, and in the poverty-stricken areas of developing countries.

Sisters have historically been involved in educational ministries ranging from day care to elementary and secondary education to higher education. Tutoring and offering General Educational Development (GED) classes to prisoners is another example of this ministry. Sisters also minister through their gifts as authors, musicians, and artists.

Ministries of advocacy on behalf of women and children, people who are poor or disabled, and refugees and immigrants are also part of furthering the mission of Christ. Other areas of advocacy include life issues such as abortion and euthanasia and environmental protection of the earth and its resources. These are only some of the areas where sisters have joined with other church and civic leaders and with all people of goodwill to end abuses to human dignity and to foster life for all of creation.

Pope Paul VI challenged all people of goodwill, "If you want peace, work for justice" *(Message for the Celebration of the Fifth World Day of Peace,* 1972). In the parable of the good Samaritan, Jesus teaches that we *are* our brothers' and sisters' keepers, regardless of their social status, religion, or cultural heritage.

Ministry is
a tangible experience
of God's love and care for all.

Aspects of Ministry

Ministry is more than a one-way street. A sister frequently finds her own life broadened and transformed through her work. Sisters do not come with all the answers or as perfect "got-it-all-together" women. They come to ministry as companions, and in this companionship they find themselves ministered to, even as they minister. This mutual flow of grace makes ministry a tangible experience of God's love and care for all, as in the following story related to me by Sister Marie, who has worked for many years in the inner city:

> Several of the sisters who lived in my local community went each Saturday night to downtown Philadelphia to feed homeless people. During the winter, we took hot tea, sandwiches, and other food items to distribute.
>
> One homeless man, whom I will call "Steve," would meet us each week and help carry the bags of food we had prepared. Several months

and many conversations later, Steve told us that he had gone to a Catholic school as a young boy. When I asked him which one, he named the school where I had taught when I first began my teaching ministry. As we talked more, I discovered that not only had he gone to this school but I had taught several of his sisters and brothers! In amazement he said to me, "You know my mother!"

As our relationship with Steve developed, we started to invite him to the convent. We asked him to dinner regularly, included him in our prayer, and celebrated his birthday with him, and he shared in many of our celebrations.

Steve eventually joined a rehabilitation program for his addiction. It was a long journey of rehab, then falling back into addiction, and then beginning rehab again. When I became discouraged with his many relapses, the sisters in my community supported and strengthened me to continue to stand with Steve as he struggled through his recovery.

Years have now gone by, and Steve is no longer on the streets, no longer an addict. He has a job, his own apartment, and a car. He still calls me several times a week and continues to visit us in the convent. He tells me he thanks God every day for the sisters, but I thank God every day for Steve.

His life remains a source of inspiration to me. When I see him reach out to someone else who is homeless or addicted, or when he visits one of our elderly sisters in our retirement home, I am awed and humbled by his goodness. He has become what Henri Nouwen describes as a "wounded healer" to others (*The Wounded Healer*). Through Steve I can "see" Christ so much more clearly and deepen my own faith. Steve helps me appreciate family and good friends—for he has neither—and he points out the gift they are to me.

Yes, I have become more faith filled, more appreciative, more aware of the needs of persons who are homeless and addicted. Truly, I am a better person because of Steve. With infinite wisdom and love, God saw that Steve and I needed each other, and so that evening many years ago on the streets of Philadelphia, our ministry to each other began.

Religious congregations "teach people how to fish" in various ways.

The proverb, "If you give people fish, they eat for a day; if you teach them how to fish, they eat for a lifetime," reflects the two aspects of ministry: taking care of immediate needs and working to change the systems and conditions that cause human suffering. Both approaches are necessary and often go hand in hand.

Religious congregations "teach people how to fish" in various ways. One approach is through literacy projects that instruct people who have inadequate reading skills. Teaching English as a second language (ESL) to adults is one example. Sisters offer classes to low-income, multiethnic, undereducated women and men so that they can find better employment, further their education, and improve the quality of life for themselves and their families. Educational programs in economically depressed rural and urban areas offer basic tutoring, GED classes, health and child care, and parenting classes.

Sisters are also involved in political activism, a key element in fostering social change. This activity includes meeting with local and state politicians and policy makers to advocate better health care for women and children, shelter and rehabilitation programs for homeless people, safety for victims of violent crimes, and programs that address issues such as domestic violence, abuse, child labor, and care for the elderly poor. Some congregations register with the United Nations as nongovernmental organizations (NGOs) and use their UN status to advocate for human rights around the world.

Members of religious congregations use their influence as educators to attempt to counteract the evils of our society, such as racism, prejudice, violence, and hatred, by introducing people to the richness of other cultures and by teaching tolerance, nonviolent conflict resolution, and the paramount need for forgiveness in everyone's life. Commitment to education at all levels and in all strata of society fosters acceptance of others and creates a more tolerant world for future generations.

On a more direct level of service, religious congregations, sometimes in collaboration with government agencies, run shelters for abused women and children that offer support, counseling, legal assistance, and job training. Sisters work with AIDS patients and their families and with those who are disabled or mentally impaired to enable them to improve their quality of life.

Sister Janice, who works with persons with disabilities, tells about her ministry:

> While I would never say it is easy to live with a disabling chronic condition like rheumatoid arthritis, having this condition has given me the privilege of being able to experience similar circumstances among the people with whom I minister. I have worked for thirteen years with people who are blind, deaf, or both, who are quadriplegic or paraplegic, who have difficulty speaking, and who suffer mental illness or mental retardation. All experience extreme marginalization from a society that has difficulty accepting them as a complete person.
>
> I have seen the determined resilience of the human spirit, for almost all the persons with a disability to whom I have ministered have come to accept and integrate the disability into their life. They refuse to be defined by limits, and they retain hope in life. Their profound message of joy and hope in what could be a despairing situation is a powerful witness to nondisabled people.
>
> Generally, my ministry involves supporting the life of persons with disabilities. This may mean referring someone who needs a wheelchair to the local disability resource center, listening to the pain of a mother who has just learned that her child has cerebral palsy, or using my skills as a spiritual director with a recently paralyzed man who is struggling to find God. Along with this support is the aspect of advocacy in helping to ensure the civil rights of disabled people under the Americans With Disabilities Act. My ministry also includes organizing disability awareness days in schools and parishes and speaking to health care professionals and church ministers to raise their awareness about disability.

I recall one particularly moving experience when I learned in a deeper way what it means to be part of the broken Body of Christ. I had helped plan a Mass for people with disabilities, and the priest who was celebrating the Mass was in a wheelchair. When the time arrived for Communion, one by one they came: Simone, a woman who is legally blind; Dan, a wheelchair user; Edna, a paraplegic woman; and a young man with Tourette's syndrome, whose outbursts ceased as he received the Eucharist. As I watched this procession, the words of Saint Paul came to mind:

> We are afflicted in every way, but not crushed; perplexed, but not driven to despair; persecuted, but not forsaken; struck down, but not destroyed; always carrying in the body the death of Jesus, so that the life of Jesus may also be made visible in our bodies. (2 Corinthians 4:8–10)

In this sacred moment I understood more profoundly the brokenness that binds Jesus to people with disabilities and the power that resides in these "earthen vessels."

To meet other needs of the Body of Christ, some congregations have provided direct assistance to needy persons by working in conjunction with the United States Department of Housing and Urban Development (HUD) to provide affordable, low-income housing for persons who are elderly or poor. Other congregations have converted space to be used for day care for children of working parents and have renovated their own buildings to be accessible to people with disabilities.

In all these many ministries, the sister brings her faith and Gospel values to her service of others. This element makes the work of a vowed religious more than just a job, a good deed, or a humanitarian effort. She imbues her ministry with the belief that God dwells in each individual and in all creation. The sacredness of the human person and of the earth is the source that animates her ministry.

Foreign missions are the focus of ministry for some congregations, such as the Maryknoll Sisters. The category of foreign missions also includes the United States of America. Sisters from other countries come to the United States and minister in inner cities, suburbs, and rural areas. The usual focus of foreign missions is on education and health care. This ministry can be extremely challenging as the sisters enter into a new culture with different traditions, practices, and languages than their own. Before going to work in a foreign country, they spend time in classes to learn about the culture, the language, and the customs of the people they will be serving.

Sometimes this ministry can be extremely dangerous. Sisters have been tortured, raped, abused, and killed because of their commitment to the Gospel and their work with the poor. In 1980, three sisters and a laywoman missionary were murdered in El Salvador. In 1989, a sister was kidnapped and tortured in Guatemala before being released by her captors. Although such extreme violence against sisters is not common and congregations do their utmost to protect their sisters, violence does happen. Then the words of Jesus become ever more real, "No one has greater love than this, to lay down one's life for one's friends" (John 15:13).

In meeting multiple ministry needs, a sister must sometimes live with members of another congregation. For example, a Dominican sister may reside with Franciscan sisters in what is known as intercongregational living. At other times a ministry need is so great that a sister must live alone to meet it. Fostering healthy relationships with other members of the church, with neighbors, and with colleagues in her ministry and keeping in communication with other sisters sustain and offer companionship and "community" for a sister living alone. Some congregations, however, do not allow their members to live with sisters of other congregations or to live alone.

There is a lighter side to ministry. Often through the friendships she makes in her ministry, a sister receives invitations to join with family members in celebrating weddings, birthdays, and anniversaries or in attending a picnic or a dinner. These occasions add a measure of pleasure and fun to the more serious aspects of ministry.

Humorous events happen in ministry, too, as the following story shows:

Teaching in Catholic schools today, sisters meet many children who are not Catholic and, therefore, are unfamiliar with the lifestyle of a sister. Frequently, they are the ones who show us God's humor and allow us to laugh at ourselves. One little girl, who had left our school to attend a boarding school, came back to visit. She was telling me about her third-grade schedule, her classes, and how students were awakened each morning. I told her I remembered that when I was a little girl, my father woke me up every morning by singing. She asked in an awed voice, "Sister Marie, was your father a nun, too?"

Countless experiences like this one bring laughter and simple joy to ministry.

The work of sisters, brothers, and priests alongside dedicated laypeople, young and old, has had untold impact in creating the world that Jesus envisioned, where no one is in need, peace reigns, and the Good News can be heard. This mission of Jesus continues today, and he still speaks these words of encouragement: "I am with you always" (Matthew 28:20).

The vow of obedience (promising to listen to God's voice), the vow of poverty (freeing sisters to respond to that voice and go where they are needed), and the vow of chastity (promising to love all without distinction) create the soil in which all ministry is planted, grows, and bears fruit.

To be the Body of Christ in the world today is the call of every Christian. The following prayer adapted from the writings of Saint Teresa of Ávila says it best:

Christ has no body now on earth but yours;
no hands but yours; no feet but yours.
It is your eyes through which Christ's compassion looks out to the
    world;
your feet with which he must walk about doing good;
your hands with which he blesses humanity;
your voice with which his forgiveness is spoken;
your heart with which he now loves.

Chapter 8

Everything You Want to Know About Sisters but Have No One to Ask

Is there a difference between a nun and a sister?

Yes, there are several differences. *Nuns* are members of contemplative congregations. The focus of their life is prayer and contemplation. Nuns pray together the liturgy of the hours, five to seven times a day. They also have times for private prayer and attend Mass in their chapel daily and on Sunday. Carmelite nuns are one example of a contemplative congregation.

Sisters are members of active, apostolic congregations. The focus of their life is service to others through their ministries. Sisters also attend daily and Sunday Mass, but it is usually in the parish church. They pray the liturgy of the hours twice a day together, morning and evening, and also take time for personal prayer.

Nuns live in monasteries and by canon law are not permitted to leave the monastery except in rare circumstances and with permission. Visits from family and friends are restricted to certain times and areas of the monastery (canon 667). Their purpose—prayer and contemplation—requires that there be no distractions from the outside world.

Sisters live in convents, with no restrictions on their comings and goings. Because they are involved in work with people, their ministries take prominence. They have no constraints in the time spent in or out of the convent. Some sisters live by themselves or with one other sister.

Nuns earn their income through some work of the monastery but within the monastery. Examples include making candy, stationery, or altar bread for Mass. Sisters earn their income through ministries, such as teaching, nursing, and social work.

The main difference between nuns and sisters is their *purpose*. For nuns it is a life dedicated to prayer for the needs of the world. For sisters it is a life of prayer dedicated to people through active ministry.

Although the term *nun* is commonly used today to describe all women with vows who live in community, this usage is incorrect. Because nuns are cloistered and rarely leave the monastery, it would be safe to assume that the women religious you see in public are sisters.

Why don't all sisters wear the habit (the religious dress)?

Each of the hundreds of different religious congregations in the United States has looked at the issue of religious dress and decided whether to remain in the traditional habit, to wear the conservative clothing of the day, or to leave the choice up to the individual sister. Congregations whose members never wore a traditional habit have no need to discuss this question. Congregations that choose to wear a habit affirm that the witness of religious dress is paramount to their identity and ministry. Congregations that choose to wear "lay clothes" believe that their members can thereby identify more closely with the people to whom they minister. These sisters usually wear a cross, a pin, or some other type of insignia that identifies them as a member of a particular congregation.

The most important aspect of a sister's life is her vowed commitment to God and to her congregation, lived in service to others.

Public opinion about sisters who wear or do not wear traditional religious dress has swung both ways. Some people are angered, hurt, or confused by the changes. Their frequent comment is, "We can't tell you apart from everyone else." Others welcome the change of dress; they feel they can now relate more easily to sisters and approach them more freely. Both views are valid. The sight of a woman in habit can inspire thoughts of God and of Christ's love and motivate the observer to be more merciful, loving, and kind. But some people feel the habit distances them from sisters, or they sense an unconscious "pedestal" effect that treats sisters as a privileged group better than other people. Ultimately, the most important aspect of a sister's life is her vowed commitment to God and to her congregation, lived in service to others.

Can sisters date?

No, they have given their lives to Christ through the promises of poverty, chastity, and obedience. They are happy in this choice and are not seeking romantic relationships with men.

Can sisters have male friendships?

Yes, and many do. How dull life would be with friends only of the same gender! Becoming a sister does not mean that the woman dislikes men or does not enjoy their company.

Do sisters ever regret not being married or not having children?

Yes, at times they wonder what marriage and being a parent might be like. Sisters are not immune to the old "what if?" question that occurs in every lifestyle. However, these thoughts do not reach the level of regret, nor do they preoccupy the sisters. They have chosen this lifestyle while knowing what they are saying yes and no to, and they are fulfilled in the choice they have made.

If a woman wants to leave religious life and stop being a sister, can she?

Yes, during the formation period, a sister is free to leave the congregation at the end of any year and not renew her vows or promises (canons 653, 688). After final vows, separation and release from these promises is a serious and complex process. In such instances she must follow a specific procedure (canons 691, 692). Because vows are not one of the seven sacraments, the church will grant a release from the vows. Relatively few women today leave religious life after final vows, but some do.

Can the congregation ask a sister to leave?

Yes, this decision results from a discussion between the sister and the congregational leadership before she makes her vows for life; in grave instances the request occurs after final vows (canons 689, 694–696). Dismissal is a serious action, never done lightly or easily. During the formation process that leads to final vows, the sister engages in regular conversation with the formation staff and also meets periodically with the congregation's leadership. Usually, the decision that religious life is "not for me" is a mutual one. The congregation and the sister both realize that this lifestyle is not suited to her personality and gifts. The woman's leave-taking is amicable, and often her convent friendships endure.

Do sisters ever argue?

Yes, disagreements and conflict are bound to occur in a group of individuals with different outlooks, opinions, and personal habits, but everyone strives to obey the call of Jesus for forgiveness and reconciliation. It is unrealistic to expect a sister to have a personal fondness for every sister she lives with, but she is expected to show respect and charity to all sisters.

Can sisters watch television, go to movies, listen to music, and go out with family and friends?

Yes, everyone's life needs a balance between work and pleasure. Learning how to keep a healthy balance of work, prayer, rest, and leisure is very important.

Can sisters keep money or other gifts that family or friends give them?

This question refers to personal gifts and money, not to funds received for ministry. A sister may accept and keep such offerings or choose to give the money or items to the congregation. Each sister must decide in her own conscience what is best in light of her promise of poverty. A sister who receives a substantial amount of money, even as a personal gift, would be expected to give it to the congregation.

What does the congregation do with the money it receives from a sister's ministry or through gifts and donations?

Pooled resources are used for the current and future needs of the sisters and their ministries. These include health care, education, housing, cars and insurance, the needs of elderly sisters, savings for future needs, spiritual renewal, theological updating, and funding of ministries that do not provide any remuneration for the congregation, such as work with the materially poor and marginalized portion of society.

Can a lesbian be accepted into a congregation and become a sister?

Yes. Although canon law does not prohibit this acceptance, individual congregations are free to decide. Most congregations today would accept a woman with this orientation, provided that she can live a life of chastity, the same as what is expected of a woman who is heterosexual. Obviously, the challenges associated with a same-sex orientation are significant, and the candidate would need to face them honestly.

Do any sisters suffer from an addiction, such as alcohol, drugs, nicotine, or food?

Yes, sisters are human and have the same possible weaknesses as everyone else. What occurs outside of religious life is also found inside. The congregation charitably and responsibly confronts sisters with addictions. They receive assistance from the congregation and from their friends to get the help they need.

Can a sister own her own car?

No, the vow of poverty forbids this. Cars are provided to sisters in the following ways:
- The convent or the congregation, through pooled resources, purchases one or more cars for the use of all the sisters.
- The parish purchases one or more cars for the use of all the sisters.
- A sister's ministry provides a car while she is in that work. Use of the car is usually restricted to the sister in the ministry.

Is there a specific time a sister must go to bed at night and get up in the morning?

No, the time she goes to bed depends on when she gets tired. The hour for rising depends on how long it takes her to get ready for the day, what time her work begins, and the hour when the community gathers for prayer.

Do family and friends address a sister by her first name or as "sister?"

Family and friends usually call a sister by her first name.

Can sisters take a vacation?

Yes, every sister has vacation time from her ministry. She might join in a family vacation or connect with other sisters or friends and enjoy time together. The vow of poverty limits the kinds and types of vacations.

(When a layperson offers a sister a shore or mountain house for some vacation time, whoops of delight resound!)

What do the initials after a sister's name mean?

The initials identify her as a member of a particular congregation. For instance, IHM identifies an Immaculate Heart of Mary sister; RSM signifies a Religious Sister of Mercy. However, the initials do not always translate exactly, as with the initials of the Dominican Sisters, OP, which stand for Order of Preachers, whose founder is Saint Dominic, renowned for his oratorical skill.

Do some sisters want to be priests?

Yes, and some laywomen would like to be ordained. The Catholic church restricts ordination to men, a policy that some lay and religious women (and men) consider discriminatory and unjust. Some women believe they have gifts that call them to ordination, but because the priesthood is exclusively for men, these women think that their talents are ignored and rejected—and they do not feel these gifts are as well suited to religious, married, or single life. Pope John Paul II has made it clear that ordination will not be open to women.

Why do so few women enter religious life today?

The answer is multifaceted; however, part of the response must be "mystery." God's plan in this situation is not clear, but the answer is not only the mystery of God's plan. There are reasons why few women become sisters today:

- In the past the only way a woman could be active in church-related work was by being a sister. In the 1960s, church ministry opened up to laypeople; as a result, work in church-related fields and in liturgical service (eucharistic minister, lector, religious educator, pastoral minister, and so on) is no longer limited to sisters.
- Another hindrance might be a choice made in young adulthood, such as getting married, having a child, that closes the door to the

religious lifestyle, or the lack of enough accurate information about this vocation for it to be a viable consideration.

- Contemporary cultural values conflict with the spiritual values of a religious vocation. The past saw little difference between the values of society and of religion. Today, the chasm is great: sexual unrestraint and exploration, the consuming desire for material possessions, staunch individualism, and the drive for power are all contrary to community living and the promises of chastity, poverty, and obedience. Religious life is a countercultural lifestyle, just like Jesus' lifestyle and message in his time. The message of Jesus and of the church is still the call to holiness for *everyone*. Regardless of their ultimate lifestyle, all persons are called to holiness of life and to a personal relationship with Jesus Christ.

- With the "graying" of religious life and the presence of fewer sisters in the ministry of education, young people today no longer have the opportunity to know sisters on a personal level. This lack of relationship, a catch-22 situation, leaves the young person with few role models to follow.

- Parents and significant others no longer encourage the choice to become a sister; the reverse is true. This lifestyle has somehow become a pariah. People who demand, "Where are all the sisters?" might ask themselves whether they have encouraged their own daughter or niece in this direction.

These are some answers for the lack of sisters in the church today. I firmly believe that God is still calling and inspiring women to say yes to this lifestyle. In order for you to consider this vocation as an option, you need to face squarely your fears and misconceptions and obtain accurate information about religious life.

Jesus said, "You will know the truth, and the truth will make you free" (John 8:32). It is my hope that as more women come to greater truth about this vocation, they will feel free to choose it.

For Further Reading

Arnold, Fritz. "Religious Obedience in a World in Search of Freedom and Maturity," *Bulletin,* no. 101, pp. 34–41. Rome: International Union of Superiors General, 1996.

Bryant, Kathy. "How to Live Celibacy Well," *Vision: The 1999 Religious Vocation Discernment Guide,* pp. 44–46. Chicago: Claretian Publications, 1999.

Code of Canon Law. Latin-English edition. Translation prepared under the auspices of the Canon Law Society of America. Washington: Canon Law Society of America, 1983.

De Maria, Richard J. "Poverty as the Embrace of Insecurity," *Review for Religious,* vol. 52, no. 3, May–June 1993, pp. 432–445.

Fiand, Barbara. *Where Two or Three Are Gathered: Community Life for the Contemporary Religious.* New York: Crossroad, 1992.

Kelley, Barbara. "The Adventures of Joining a Religious Community," *Vision: The 1999 Religious Vocation Discernment Guide,* pp. 27–31. Chicago: Claretian Publications, 1999.

Kovats, Alexandra. "Reflections on the Vows from a Cosmic/Ecological Perspective," *InFormation,* Religious Formation Conference, no. 146, November–December 1992, pp. 1–4.

McDermott, Rose. "Evangelical Poverty and the Vowed Life," *Religious Life Review,* vol. 36, November–December 1997, pp. 357–367.

Merkle, Judith A. *A Different Touch: A Study of Vows in Religious Life.* Collegeville, MN: Liturgical Press, 1998.

———. "Gathering the Fragments: New Times for Obedience," *Review for Religious,* vol. 55, no. 3, May–June 1996, pp. 264–282.

National Coalition for Church Vocations. "Sixteen Questions About Church Vocations," *Vision: The 1999 Religious Vocation Discernment Guide,* pp. 64–68. Chicago: Claretian Publications, 1999.

Pable, Martin. "Skills Needed for Celibacy," *Review for Religious,* vol. 57, no. 3, May–June 1998, pp. 275–285.

Rexing, Rose Mary. "How to Cope with Transition into Religious Life," *Vision: The 1999 Religious Vocation Discernment Guide,* pp. 80–83. Chicago: Claretian Publications, 1999.

Senior, Donald. "Living in the Meantime: Biblical Foundations for Religious Life," in *Living in the Meantime: Concerning the Transformation of Religious Life,* pages 55–72. Edited by Paul J. Philibert. New York: Paulist Press, 1994.

Svoboda, Melanie. "Consecrated Celibacy as Means, Peril, and Delight," *Review for Religious,* vol. 56, no. 1, January–February 1997, pp. 67–71.

Acknowledgments *(continued from page 4)*

The Scripture quotations contained herein are from the New Revised Standard Version of the Bible: Catholic Edition. Copyright © 1993 and 1989 by the Division of Christian Education of the National Council of the Churches of Christ in the USA. All rights reserved.

The quote on pages 13–14 is from "The Road Not Taken," by Robert Frost, in *The Poetry of Robert Frost* edited by Edward Connery Lathem, page 131. Copyright © 1944 by Robert Frost. Copyright © 1916, 1969 by Henry Holt and Company. Reprinted by permission of Henry Holt and Co., LLC.

The material on pages 27, 28, 28–29, 36, 38–39, 48, 72, and 75 is from the *Code of Canon Law,* Latin-English edition, translation prepared under the auspices of the Canon Law Society of America (Washington: Canon Law Society of America, 1983). Copyright © 1983 by the Canon Law Society of America, Inc. All rights reserved.

The anecdote from the Jewish tradition cited on page 29 is from *Weston Priory Bulletin,* Fall–Winter 1998. Copyright © 1998 by the Benedictine Foundation of the State of Vermont, Inc.

The quote on page 31 is from "Living in the Meantime: Biblical Foundations for Religious Life," by Donald Senior, CP, in *Living in the Meantime: Concerning the Transformation of Religious Life,* edited by Paul J. Philibert, OP (New York: Paulist Press, 1994), page 62. Copyright © 1994 by the Conference of Major Superiors of Men's Institutes of the United States. All rights reserved.

The quote on page 36 is from the Constitutions of the Sisters of Saint Joseph, Chestnut Hill, Philadelphia, as approved by the Congregation for Religious and Secular Institutes, 15 October 1987.

The material on page 39 is adapted from "Vow Series: Poverty," an address by Amata Miller, IHM, at Cardinal Dougherty High School, Philadelphia, PA, 21 November 1998.

The quote on page 50 is from "The Hound of Heaven," by Francis Thompson, in *Poems of Francis Thompson* (New York: The Century Co., 1932), page 81. Copyright © 1932 by the Century Co. All rights reserved.

The quote on page 65 is from *Message for the Celebration of the Fifth World Day for Peace,* by Pope Paul VI, 1 January 1972.

The reference on page 66 is to *The Wounded Healer: Ministry in Contemporary Society,* by Henri J. M. Nouwen (Garden City, NY: Doubleday, 1972). Copyright © 1972 by Henri J. M. Nouwen. All rights reserved.

The quotation on page 71 is a prayer said to be adapted from the writings of Saint Teresa of Ávila. The prayer card provides no further information. One possible source is Soliloquy #11, which conveys something of the same sentiment. The Soliloquies are found at the end of volume 1 of *The Collected Works of Saint Teresa of Ávila*, translated by Kieran Kavanaugh and Otilio Rodríguez (Washington: Institute of Carmelite Studies, 1976). John Michael Talbot composed a different version of "Saint Teresa's Prayer" for his album of songs, *Troubadour for the Lord* (1996).

The material in chapter 8 is adapted in part from "16 Questions About Church Vocations," by the National Coalition for Church Vocations, in *Vision: The 1999 Religious Vocation Discernment Guide,* an annual publication of the National Religious Vocation Conference (Chicago: Claretian Publications, 1999).